BORN FREE FOUNDATION

Leopard Rescue

True-Life Stories

Leopard Rescue

True-Life Stories

Written by
Sara Starbuck

First edition for the United States published in 2017
by Barron's Educational Series, Inc.

All inquiries should be addressed to:
Barron's Educational Series, Inc.
250 Wireless Boulevard
Hauppauge, New York 11788
www.barronseduc.com

Library of Congress Control Number: 2016950878
ISBN: 978-1-4380-0988-9

Date of Manufacture: January 2017
Manufactured by: RRD Shenzhen, Shenzhen, Guangdong, China

Printed in China
9 8 7 6 5 4 3 2 1

Photo copyright ©Maria Slough

Hello everyone,

I wonder what you feel when you think of a leopard? Are you frightened, struck by its beauty, fascinated by its nature—perhaps more secretive than other "big cats"?

Although I am now deeply interested in all animals, I was introduced to the wildlife world when my husband, Bill Travers, and I went to Kenya 52 years ago. We were going to be in a film called *Born Free*. It was based on a famous book by Joy Adamson and was the story of Joy, her husband George, and an orphaned lion cub called Elsa. When she was old enough, they taught Elsa to be a wild lion again, and so she was eventually able to live a natural life, hunting, mating, and having her own cubs.

When filming was over, we went on a safari and saw many other wild animals, including leopards. Over all the years that followed I have often seen them—sleeping high up in a tree, stalking their prey, with young cubs. This, of course, is how wild animals should live, free to fulfill their natural behavior. But it is not always what happens.

Thirty-two years ago, together with our eldest son, Will, we started a little group called Zoo Check which, a few years later, changed its name to the Born Free Foundation. The reason we began this work was because we had seen hundreds of wild animals living in captivity, not in the wild, and often in very restricted and pitiful circumstances.

The small zoo in Limassol, Cyprus, was such a place. Bill, who spent the last years of his life filming and photographing such zoos, visited Limassol in 1990. What he found horrified him. In 1994, I went to the zoo myself. The elephant I had seen there previously (and persuaded the zoo owner to have some shade erected for) had died, the bears had been rehomed, and the conditions for the primates were very inadequate, but not as terrible as when Bill was there. The zoo had now decided to only keep smaller animals, which gave us the opportunity to take the leopards to our Big Cat Rescue Centre in South Africa. The animals' lives would be changed forever. To my delight the brilliant author and friend of Born Free, Lauren St. John, was going to be with us on the journey, and the wonderful actress Ruth Wilson was to join us in London, then take part in the release of the leopards into their new, large, natural enclosures at Shamwari. I wish Bill could have been there to share this exciting and hopeful day.

You can imagine, I am sure, what it feels like to take wild animals from a concrete cage and introduce them to a home under African skies, where they can feel the wind, walk on the grass, hide from view if they so wish, and hear the sounds of other wild creatures. For all of us watching, it was unbelievably moving. Life, at last.

Virginia McKenna

Virginia McKenna OBE
Actress and Founder Trustee, Born Free Foundation

This is the story of the Limassol leopards, a family born behind bars, far from their natural homeland. It's a story of a rescue spanning almost twenty years, a tale of faith and courage, hardship and hope.

Leda

FACTFILE

- Born in 1990, in Tel Aviv Zoo, Israel
- Arrival at Limassol Zoo—not known
- Confident and brave
- A good mother
- Has caught birds that wandered into her enclosure
- Likes sleeping on top of her platform and looking over the reserve

Rhea

FACTFILE

- Daughter of Leda and Zeus
- Born January 1998, Limassol Zoo, Cyprus
- Shy and nervous of people
- Strong territorial instincts
- Likes sleeping on or in a large wooden box in her hospital camp

FACT FILE

Learn a new leopard fact every time you see me.

Chapter One

January 1998
Limassol Zoo, Greece

It was early morning at Limassol Zoo in Cyprus. The pale January sun had yet to rise over the Troodos Mountains. Many of the zoo's animals were already awake, making the most of the peace and quiet before the visitors arrived to point, taunt, and stare. There was a variety of birds and beasts from all over the world. The animals were crammed into pens, glass boxes, and cages that were nothing like the jungles, forests, and savannas of their natural habitats. They were bored and unhappy.

Things in the leopard cage were more cheerful. Sisters Roxanni and Rhea were only a few days old and weighed no more than a box of breakfast cereal between them! They had been given the names of legendary Greek goddesses, but they had a lot of growing to do before they would look the part. Right now, they were tiny and utterly helpless, their eyes still tightly closed.

FACT FILE

Newborn leopard cubs are born "blind," opening their eyes after about 10 days. Their eyes are blue at birth and gradually change to the piercing golden-green color that gives adults their mesmerizing stare.

Their father, Zeus, sat back, watching with little interest from the enclosure next door but their devoted mother, Leda, lay with her paws stretched out in front of her, like a sphinx, as her cubs wriggled and tumbled around. They had pink noses and soft, smoky gray coats. You could barely see their spots, although their pattern would soon become more visible.

Every few minutes, Leda decided it was time to clean her daughters again, licking them with her enormous tongue. In captivity, mothers will occasionally reject their babies, but it was obvious to everyone that Leda adored her little brood.

Kris Wiktor/Shutterstock.com

Neither Leda nor Zeus had ever seen the forest. The only trees in their enclosure were painted on the concrete-covered walls. They'd spent their entire lives prowling around undersized cages. They'd never felt the damp earth beneath their paws, or seen the open sky above them.

They didn't have anything to help them feel like true leopards: the vast spaces of "big sky" country, with its fierce sun and shady trees to hide in, the thrill of the hunt, or territory of their own to defend. And now their cubs would grow up behind bars, too.

The sun finally peaked over the Troodos Mountains and it was breakfast time at last. The crowds of noisy humans would be here soon. The animals of Limassol Zoo retreated into the shadows.

Chapter Two

The 1990s

It was 1990 when the Born Free Foundation's Founders, Virginia McKenna and her husband, Bill Travers, first became aware of the conditions at Limassol Zoo. Letters of concern were beginning to arrive, and when the animal welfare organization Animal Responsibility Cyprus (ARC) got in touch, Born Free knew the situation must be urgent. But the path ahead of them was littered with obstacles.

Limassol Zoo was built back in 1956. People knew less about the needs of animals in those days and some of the zoos of the time consisted of little more than concrete boxes with iron bars. It would be years before people realized the harm they were doing to the animals by keeping them in such conditions. Over time, the shape of zoos began to change—in appearance, at least. Glass walls and electric fences were used instead of bars to give an illusion of space and freedom, but for the animals the boundaries remained. Some of the big cats and other predators were given larger enclosures where they could experience the changing weather and feel grass underfoot but, even with these improvements, most captive conditions are a far cry from the wild.

By the early 1990s, Bill Travers had traveled across much of Europe filming evidence of suffering and neglect in hundreds of so-called "slum zoos." Of them all, the conditions that he found in Limassol Zoo were particularly bad, especially for the primates and the larger carnivores like the leopards. In the wild, these powerful predators love to stalk, run, and climb, and will roam for many miles as they hunt. They're among the fastest animals on earth, but at Limassol the leopards' cage was too small for anything other than relentless pacing.

Leopards can run as fast as 35 miles per hour.

FACT FILE

Joseph D. Anthony/Shutterstock.com

When wild animals are imprisoned in undersized cages or unsuitable enclosures, they can begin to act strangely. For example, bears and big cats who are suffering from boredom and stress will pace up and down endlessly. In fact, it is so common for big cats to exhibit this behavior in captivity that some zoos lay concrete paths around their perimeter fences to stop a trench from forming along well-worn routes. Birds will pluck out their feathers and primates will pull out their hair, hugging their knees and rocking back and forth like scared children. Bill Travers called this animal madness "Zoochosis." He used the footage of suffering animals that he filmed to make a TV documentary called "The Zoochotic Report," which was shown around the world, and began to change the way people thought about traditional zoos.

Bill Travers was desperate to see Limassol closed. But in the early 1990s, when Born Free began urging the Cypriot authorities to take action, they knew they had a long road ahead of them. Sadly, Bill died in 1994. He didn't get to see his dream of freedom for the neglected animals of Limassol. But his passion and hard work had set the wheels in motion. The Born Free team were on the case.

Chapter Three

May 1998
Limassol Zoo, Greece

It was midday and the sun was high in the cloudless sky. The air shimmered in the harsh, windless heat. At the zoo, the animals were feeling grouchy. They'd spent the morning following tiny patches of shade around their cages as the sun moved across the heavens but now there was no escape from the glare. The metal bars of their cages were too hot to rub against and their water bowls were bone dry.

Roxanni and Rhea were now four months old. They were pouncing on everything in sight. Like all young cats, leopard cubs like to play, stalk, and chase.

The playful nature of young cubs is important to ensure that they develop strong muscles and agility—it allows them to practice their reactions and to become confident in their skills. These skills are put to good use when the cubs learn to hunt.

People had been clustering around the leopard cage all morning. The cubs were a huge hit with the visitors, as they swatted with their paws and playfully gnawed at each other's limbs. Their father, Zeus, was cat-napping beside the painted forest wall, all four legs lolling to one side. His throat throbbed with the heat.

Leda was exhausted by the heat too, but the twins wouldn't let her sleep. They chased and leapt, tumbled, bit, and continually bothered her. She bowed her head forward but there was no peace to be had. Roxanni butted against her face for attention, while Rhea began playing with her mom's tail, catching it and biting down hard.

It was no use; sleep would have to wait. Leda sat up and started to lick the cubs' heads again. In the wild, Roxanni and Rhea would have had a natural playground to keep them busy, a massive climbing frame of trees and fallen branches, and plenty of space to run and hide. Instead, their "playground" was drawn on the concrete wall of their small cage. All they could do was stare at the peeling paint and perhaps dream of freedom.

Leopards are built for climbing. Their powerful muscles help to push them up as they climb. Their claws dig deep into the trees' bark, providing maximum grip, the way spiked shoes help propel an athlete along a running track. Their tails are about the same length as their lean bodies, giving them excellent balance. Leopards use the treetops for safety and to store their food.

A single leopard wouldn't stand much of a chance against a lion or a pack of hyenas, so they use their amazing climbing skills to their advantage. After making a kill they frequently hoist their prey up into a tree, out of reach of other less agile predators. Then they return whenever they want to, sometimes over the course of several days, for a delicious meal. Their ability to reach such a lofty vantage point also means that leopards often choose to hunt from above. In the shadowy trees, their spotted coats allow them to blend with the leaves and branches.

Visitors to the zoo continued to gather around the leopard cage and Leda fixed them with a cold, green, unblinking stare. Her fur bristled and her ears flattened against her head. There was nowhere for her to hide her precious cubs and the constant attention of the visitors was making her feel anxious.

Wild leopards are shy creatures; they are secretive, cautious, and wary of humans. They usually keep to themselves, lurking in the dense canopy of trees, prowling through thick bush, or skirting rocky hills, called kopjes. They emerge from the undergrowth to hunt late in the afternoon or sometimes after sunset.

A leopardess will leave her young cubs for up to 36 hours while hunting and feeding before returning to suckle them. She brings solid food to her cubs when they're about six weeks old and weans them at around three months. After about a year, they are ready to take down animals as big as small antelopes.

FACT FILE

At last, the chattering group that had gathered around the leopards' cage moved on and Leda relaxed. Her cubs had managed to squirm away from her attempt to clean them.

Leda yawned and nestled her head in her paws. The twins seemed to have calmed down. Perhaps now she'd get away with that nap.

Chapter Four

The 2000s

The release of Bill Travers' explosive documentary, "The Zoochotic Report," had a huge impact on the public's attitude to zoos. The change it started led directly to the creation of a new European law, the EU Zoos Directive. The EU, or "European Union," is a large group of European countries whose governments work together and agree to the same rules. Appalled by the conditions in some zoos, the EU made it clear that traditional zoos were no longer acceptable environments for captive animals. From now on, zoo owners would have a responsibility to house their animals in conditions as close to their natural habitat as was practically possible in the interests of conservation. In other words, when the law came into effect in 2002, it became illegal for zoo animals in any EU country to be locked away in cramped, uncomfortable cages that did not permit the animals to carry out most of their natural behaviors.

At least, that was the idea. To this day, many EU zoos have yet to meet the minimum standards required by the Directive. In Cyprus then, despite the EU ruling—and relentless pressure from Born Free and the animal welfare group, ARC—the pace of change was frustratingly slow. Limassol's local authorities were in no hurry to force the closure of an attraction, which, however completely inadequate and old-fashioned, still made money for the city. And there were the zoo workers to consider as well. Nobody wanted to lose their job. But the city couldn't afford to rebuild the zoo and comply with the law.

By now, Roxanni and Rhea were two years old. They weren't gangly, fluffy cubs anymore. They were sleek young adults with thick golden fur, covered with dense black spots; the perfect camouflage for the dappled light in the scrub of their natural homeland.

A leopard's spots are called "rosettes" because their shape is similar to that of a rose.

FACT FILE

Appstock/Shutterstock.com

In the wild, the twins would have left their mother by this point to make it on their own. Leopards usually set off to fend for themselves just before their second birthday and, unlike lions and cheetahs who stay in prides or groups, they live solitary lives except when they are raising young. Without a family or pride to back them up, leopards hunt alone, slinking through the shadows and surviving, thanks to their stealth and intelligence.

Male leopards take no part in raising their cubs. It would have been left to Leda to teach Rhea and Roxanni the skills they would need to survive without her, like hunting, climbing, and hiding in the shadows. She would have taught them how to kill prey with one swift, powerful bite, just as her own mother once taught her. Only after mastering these vital lessons would the twins be ready to set out on their own.

And yet, however much they prepared and learned with their mother, one sad fact remained. At the age of two, Roxanni and Rhea were still stuck in their small cage.

Chapter Five

January 2006
Limassol Zoo, Greece

It was a stormy January night in Limassol city. Thunder rolled over the Troodos Mountains as lightning licked at the peaks. The Mediterranean Sea crashed on the shore and clouds as black as smoke blanked out the stars. The animals at the zoo were restless and scared. Rain lashed their cages and the wind howled through the bars from every direction.

Leda and her little family were looking particularly sorry for themselves. Roxanni and Rhea were crouching together in a nervous huddle. A leopard's hearing is about five times as sensitive as a human's, so the storm was terrifyingly loud for them. Their fur was standing on end and their ears were drawn back in fear. Leda, on the other hand, was furious with the noisy, uncomfortable weather.

Zeus was slumped miserably in the corner of his cage. His arthritis—a condition that made the joints of his skeleton swell painfully—was made worse by the damp weather and the cold concrete floor. He ached all over. Every now and then he would lift his head, and move his body, trying to relieve the pain in his joints, but it was no use. It was only getting worse.

Leopards are remarkable athletes, able to swim across rivers, leap 20 ft (6 m) in a single bound, and jump 10 ft (3 m) straight up.

FACT FILE

nattanan726/Shutterstock.com

Apart from the cold and the damp, the whole leopard family was bored, and they were also getting fat. In the wild they would have had to hunt for their food, but all there ever was to do at Limassol was sleep, groom, eat, and gain weight.

Their bellies were bulging, their fur was dull and their golden-green eyes—meant for spotting prey in the long grass—were glazed over and lifeless. Things had been changing in Limassol of late, but it was all happening too slowly for the helpless leopard family. After years of promises and delays, the Cypriot authorities had agreed that the outdated, prison-like conditions at the zoo were unsuitable for keeping wild animals. The attraction had been marked for closure. But that left the problem of what to do with the animals.

It would be great to think that leopards like Leda and her family could be released into the wild, to enjoy the freedom that was their birthright, but sadly that's not a realistic option for many animals that have been in captivity for a long time. It's extremely hard to rehabilitate captive leopards that have never learned to hunt or fend for themselves. Without the survival lessons their mother would have passed on to them in the wild, they'd struggle to feed themselves and would do poorly in territorial fights. And that's assuming they were healthy and young. Rescued animals are often old or injured, making their release into the wild impossible. However, if Born Free is able to rescue them, the charity can then search for safe, comfortable new homes for leopards like Leda and her family. These homes are as close to their natural environment as possible, with huge, spacious bush enclosures, free of the dangers that they would face in the wild but suited to a leopard's lifestyle.

As Limassol Zoo's closure loomed, Born Free and ARC were eager to move the entire leopard family to Born Free's Big Cat Rescue Centre in South Africa. Life at the Centre would mean having territory of their own, where they could live out their days in comfort. But Limassol's authorities were reluctant to let their leopards go. And while they argued it out, Zeus's arthritis was growing worse. As the months passed, his pain became so constant that he barely moved from his spot in the corner of the cage.

Chapter Six

August 2008
Limassol Zoo, Greece

Leda crouched low, drawing back her lips. Ears flat and her tail down, ready to attack. Before Roxanni knew what was happening, her mother launched herself forward like a fur-covered missile. Roxanni caught the movement at the last moment and dodged to one side. Rhea jumped in to join the fight, pouncing on her sister from behind. The three big cats became a single tumbling ball of teeth and claws, rolling and biting on the floor of their cage.

Rhea tried to clamp down on her sister's neck, but sank her teeth into her ear instead. Roxanni backed away to hide in the corner, snarling a warning to her sister not to follow. She watched the other two cautiously, her tail flicking back and forth angrily. The others had been attacking her more and more recently and the cage they shared was not a happy place to be. As Rhea and Leda started to calm down and catch their breath, they eyed Roxanni cautiously.

It was just the three of them now. Zeus had died in the spring. His arthritis was so painful that he could hardly move and was even reluctant to eat and drink. It was clear to the zoo's vets that he was not responding to treatment, so the decision was made to put him down.

In the end, Zeus spent his whole life in a small cage. He never got to sleep under the vast African sky or run, or hunt, or climb. He never got to be a proper leopard at all.

The average life span of a wild leopard is between 11–13 years.

As time went on, Leda and Rhea began to bully Roxanni. In the wild, Leda would have left her daughters to fend for themselves long ago and the unnatural confinement was taking its toll. A future Born Free veterinary inspection would reveal Roxanni had potential health problems, which may also explain Leda and Rhea's behavior.

Roxanni grew timid and withdrawn. Her mother and sister would snarl and lash out at her every day until, in the end, the zoo had to separate them. Leda and Rhea lived together in one half of the cage and Roxanni lived alone in the other half.

Roxanni started chewing and sucking on the end of her tail until its once magnificent tip was completely raw and bald.

On the other side of the cage, Leda and Rhea weren't doing much better. Leda had taken to sitting in Zeus's old spot in the corner for hours on end while Rhea padded back and forth in front of her. Back and forth. Back and forth. All day, every day.

The team at Born Free were still waiting for the go-ahead to move the leopards to their African home, but yet another hold-up had developed. That Easter, an illegal shipment of exotic animals had arrived in Limassol. At first, the local authorities tried to prevent the ship carrying them from entering Cypriot territory, but in the end they had no choice but to allow it to land. The law said that the Cypriot Veterinary Services were supposed to confiscate the animals, but they had nowhere to put them except for the cramped cages of Limassol Zoo.

So, while Born Free was busy raising money to find homes for Limassol's animals, the zoo was still filling up with new arrivals!

Time passed and Roxanni withdrew even more. She went off her food, and started to look thin and weak. Every time she moved she would let out a growl or a hiss, as if something was hurting her. It was beginning to look like none of the leopards were ever going to get to Africa.

Chapter Seven

May 2009
Limassol Zoo, Greece

At long last, after years of campaigning by Born Free and ARC, Limassol's authorities admitted that there simply wasn't enough room at their small city zoo to look after large wild animals. The battle was finally won.

Meanwhile, Roxanni was still unwell. Blood tests had revealed a kidney problem. She was now receiving treatment and after a check-up from the vets, it was decided that she was well enough to cope with the long journey to South Africa. The date was set. Life for the three leopards was about to change.

It was just after dawn on May 30th, 2009, when their voyage to Africa began. Ribbons of scrappy, pink clouds criss-crossed the sky and the roads of the city were still empty. The first members of the rescue team began to arrive and gathered around the leopards' cage, discussing the job at hand. This was the day they had all been waiting and planning for. Leda, Rhea, and Roxanni gazed back at these unfamiliar humans warily and yawned. Rhea slunk over to the edge of the cage and eyed the newcomers suspiciously. Her tail flicked from side to side as she sized them up.

Soon to arrive was Born Free's Senior Veterinary Consultant, John Knight. It was his job to sedate the animals with darts so they could be treated for parasites, as required by the permits, and safely loaded into their crates. The leopards had been shut in different sections of their enclosure so a sleeping leopard was not at risk of being attacked by another. Leda was to be darted first. John crept toward her cage, quietly. He lifted his blow pipe and, with a puff of his cheeks, a tranquilizer dart shot out and lodged right in the muscle of Leda's hind leg. It was a great shot. Leda gave a weak snarl and staggered then collapsed heavily onto her side as she lost consciousness. One down, two to go. But the twins would be trickier. They'd seen what happened to Leda and were anxious about what was going on.

It took a while to sedate the nervous younger leopards, but once all three of them were asleep, Tony Wiles, Born Free's Big Cat Rescue Consultant, helped John to move them to their traveling crates. Once safely inside, the vet reversed the sedative and the mesh shutters were quickly slid into place. It is not safe to transport a sedated animal in case they are sick while asleep or have trouble breathing. Leda, Rhea, and Roxanni had to be fully awake on the long journey to their new home. By the time the sun had inched over the horizon, they were finally on their way to Africa.

The Born Free convoy, ten dedicated workers from the charity, including Virginia McKenna herself, first carried their big cat cargo to Paphos Airport, with a VIP police escort riding alongside to help them through the early morning traffic. From there, they flew to London's Gatwick Airport on a flight generously donated by the travel company, Thomson Airways. Then they were driven across town to Heathrow Airport to catch a connecting flight to Johannesburg in South Africa.

By the time they reached Heathrow, word of the leopards' arrival had spread. The press, as well as a group of curious airport employees, crowded around the loading bay to get a glimpse of the travelers. John Knight lifted the shutters to check the leopards' condition. Rhea and Leda crouched low in their crates and glared out. A newspaper photographer stepped forward to take a photograph and Roxanni let out a snarl. The fierce sound vibrated around her crate as she curled back her lips to reveal her teeth. The onlookers fell silent and backed away at once.

FACT FILE

Leopards have a distinctive call that sounds like a wooden plank being cut with a coarse saw. They growl when angry and purr when they are happy and relaxed. They can also snarl, cough, puff, grunt, spit, and rasp.

Soon, the leopards and the team were on a British Airways flight to Johannesburg, South Africa. Leda and the twins were hungry, but they couldn't be given any food in case they were sick. Their stomachs were rumbling but at least their water bowls were full. And there would be fresh meat waiting for them when they got to the Centre. As the plane climbed through the clouds, the captain announced his leopard cargo to his human passengers, promising—for any nervous flyers—that they were securely locked away. "Lion Bars" were handed out to every passenger to celebrate the leopards' freedom … they were made with chocolate, of course!

From time to time, as the long flight went on, John or Tony would go into the hold to check on Leda and the twins, squeezing down the narrow shaft from the cabin into the dark storage space where the crates were packed. Whenever they shone their torches through the breathing holes in the crates, they could see the leopards' shining eyes watching them, completely unaware they were 30,000 feet up in the air. The journey was uneventful, but it was still a relief when they touched down at last. They'd made it to Africa.

Now, the Born Free team had Customs to deal with. Importing a leopard takes a lot of paperwork and everything had to be checked by the South African authorities. The airport was a noisy place, with fork-lift trucks beeping and workers calling out to each other loudly. Normally, the leopards would have waited there overnight for their connecting flight onward, but the company that had helped to arrange their Customs clearance, Air Alternative Africa, had kindly allowed the leopards to be housed in their quiet warehouse instead.

After a few hours sleep, the leopards were loaded onto another plane—generously provided by the international courier company Express Air—for their final flight to Port Elizabeth in the Eastern Cape. It was a much shorter flight than the last one and when they reached the airport, the Centre team from

Shamwari were there to meet them. This was the tenth time that Born Free had delivered rescued big cats to Shamwari and so it was a happy reunion for everyone there.

The three crates containing Leda and the twins were loaded carefully onto the backs of three separate pick-up trucks and they set off on the forty-minute drive to Shamwari. As they left Port Elizabeth, the buildings faded away and the empty road stretched out before them, winding through scrubland, framed by craggy mountains. The light was dazzling and the smells of wood smoke and red dust filled the air. The leopards were quiet and still, sitting as far back in the semi-darkness as they could manage. Little did they know what was waiting for them.

Chapter Eight

June 1, 2009
Shamwari Reserve, South Africa

As the late morning sun rose in the sky, the Limassol leopards arrived at their new home, Shamwari. In Shona, a language spoken by some of the local people, "shamwari" means "friend," and many animals have come to learn that the people who work there are just that … friends.

Born Free has two securely-fenced Big Cat Rescue Centres within Shamwari's award-winning "Big Five" wildlife reserve, places where rescued animals who don't have the ability to survive on their own can enjoy a life as close to the wild as possible.

For Leda and her grown-up daughters, a special three-acre plot had been reserved at the Jean Byrd Centre in the north of Shamwari. Thick with acacia and thorn trees, it was beautiful.

Leopards are carnivores and eat any meat item they can find. Rats, antelope, monkeys, fish… bugs, anything they can get their paws on. They are as happy to scavenge a meal as to hunt one.

FACT FILE

It had been decided that Leda would be released first. By now she was nineteen years old, which is quite old for a leopard, but Leda was as fit as a fiddle. Virginia McKenna climbed on top of Leda's crate, ready to open the door. Nearby stood Shamwari's vet, Dr. Johan Joubert, the rest of the Shamwari team, the Born Free rescue team, and a collection of journalists and photographers from the local and international press. The photographers' camera shutters clicked and people muttered excitedly. After such a long fight for the leopards' freedom, it was an important moment. While Bill Travers couldn't be there to celebrate the victory that he had worked so hard for, he was there in spirit. The love he had for his friends—animal and human—his family and his cause could be felt. Years earlier, Bill's love had started the Limassol leopards down the long road to freedom. Now it was time for Virginia to finish the job.

Before moving to their permanent home, the leopards would first be released into the three smaller hospital "camps" or enclosures that adjoined it. They wouldn't be let out into the full enclosure until the vets and Born Free team were sure they were fit and ready, but even these smaller enclosures were dramatically different from the conditions they were used to back in Limassol.

Cautiously, Virginia eased up the door of Leda's crate while the assembled crowd held their breath. Nothing happened! Leda did just the opposite of what everyone wanted her to do. She sat stone still. Beyond her crate was a thick strip of trees and beyond it the broad grassland, filled with the rustlings and rumblings of the wild. The whole world was calling out to her. But then there were the humans, standing there, watching. Leda could see them through the little air holes in her crate. Every instinct said danger. She wasn't going to budge an inch.

Ten minutes later Leda was still in her crate. Everyone else waited as patiently as possible. The press had been warned; you can't hurry a big cat.

Another five minutes passed. Then, suddenly, Leda bolted straight out of her crate. Keeping low to the ground, she charged straight for the cover of a wild camphor bush and dived under it. Her dash for freedom was so fast that most of the photographers who'd been waiting to take her picture missed their chance completely.

Next out of the crates was Roxanni. She was the most timid of the three leopards and had been the unhappiest at Limassol. Roxanni stuck her head out gingerly; the fluffy white underside of her chin tipped up toward the sky and caught the sun. For a moment she stared out across the waving grass. She could feel the breeze ruffling her fur. She sniffed the air, taking in the smells of wild Africa, and tilted her head to listen to the new and exciting sounds. One cautious paw followed another, then Roxanni sprang from her crate and raced toward the wooden shelter that had been prepared for her.

There was no messing around with Rhea. The moment the door of her crate was opened, she made a bold leap for freedom, dashing over to the nearest bit of scrub and crouching low to the ground as she tried to make herself as small as possible.

Virginia and the team relaxed at last. They hugged and congratulated one another, delighted it had all gone so well. They would need to stay for a few days to monitor the leopards' progress—but so far, the signs were all looking good.

In time, the Limassol leopards would come to love their home. They would be the mistresses of all they surveyed, proud, capable, and strong. But right now, all three of them felt small and vulnerable. Everything was different, and there was certainly a lot for them to get used to. But they would soon become part of it all—this beautiful, breathtaking new world.

Chapter Nine

June 7, 2009
Shamwari Reserve, South Africa

Roxanni was sitting on the roof of the shelter in her hospital camp, stargazing. The moon was so bright that you could see the colors of the flowers and the bright red fruit of the Num Num tree. Far beyond the perimeter of the enclosure, the roars of Shamwari's wild lions echoed around the valley, and the choir of night-time insects sang. It was a wonderfully noisy night. Roxanni dropped her gaze and spotted Rhea, sitting near the fence between their separate hospital "camp" enclosures. Roxanni yawned, exposing her fearsome teeth, and jumped gracefully down from the roof.

Her landing was quiet, the impact absorbed by the thick padded soles of her paws. Slowly, the sisters had started walking side by side in the moonlight, divided only by the chain-link fence between their enclosures.

FACT FILE

The thick pads that are under a leopard's paws are like a cushion. They allow the leopard to move very quietly and also act as shock absorbers for running and jumping. Hidden between the pads and fur are the leopard's claws, tucked away safely until they are needed.

Rhea was listening to the night. Small nocturnal creatures rustled in the bushes nearby, arousing her hunter's instinct. But she'd eaten a lot of antelope meat earlier in the day, so, for now at least, she was still. There was fresh blood to be licked off her long white whiskers.

Leopards use their long, sensitive whiskers like a radar. They can help the leopard feel its way in the dark or when walking through tall grass. The whiskers face forward when the leopard is walking and are angled back when it is sniffing something. They stick out sideways when the leopard is resting.

Leda was over in her own part of the leopard enclosure by a sturdy tree, scratching the bark, something she hadn't been able to do properly on the dry old tree trunk at Limassol.

A leopard's strong, very sharp, curved claws are fully retractable.

Leda stretched out her body, arching her spine as she dug her claws into the soft surface of the fig tree. Leda had been spending most of the day tucked away in her cave. At night, she would emerge to prowl around under cover of darkness. She had never had anywhere to hide before and now that she could vanish from sight whenever she wished, she was taking full advantage. When the keepers brought her meat, she would wait until they left before racing out to grab the carcass, without stopping, and drag it swiftly to her refuge to eat. She slept there, too. It was probably the first place that Leda had ever felt safe.

All three leopards quickly adjusted and had become happier and more relaxed. They no longer slunk about, close to the ground, but walked upright, with their tails held high. They were eating well, too. Four pounds (2 kg) of good red meat, three times a week, instead of every day, just like the eating pattern of leopards in the wild. Soon it would be time to take down the internal fences and find out how the family reacted when they were together.

Chapter Ten

June 19, 2009
Shamwari Reserve, South Africa

At long last, following a careful inspection by
Shamwari's veterinary assistant, Dr. Murray Stokoe,
they decided to try putting the leopards together
in one enclosure. Born Free and Shamwari knew
this would not be without risk. When animals that
are solitary by nature are shut together in small
enclosures, such as a zoo or circus trailer, they endure
each other's company to avoid the risk of injury—
though they may fight even then. Born Free knew that
Leda and Rhea had already ganged up on Roxanni

in Limassol. There was a chance that, given all the space they had at Shamwari, it would stimulate their territorial instincts. On the other hand, with room to get away from each other and lots of bushes and undergrowth for privacy, everyone was hoping that the peace between them would continue.

As usual, Roxanni and Rhea were sitting close together, right alongside each other, separated only by the thin fence. With Leda tucked away in her cat-cave, it seemed like a good time to try releasing her daughters. First the outer gates, then the inner gates were opened …

By that time it was early afternoon. Rather than venturing straight out, the first thing Roxanni and Rhea did was to swap camps! After a good sniff around each other's territory, they met in the middle to growl at each other. Roxanni's growls were louder and she now seemed to be the more dominant of the two. Fortunately, the growls didn't turn into a scrape and, after a while, Rhea stalked off to the outer ring of the enclosure. Roxanni was in no hurry to conquer this new territory. Instead, she lay outside Leda's camp, grumbling.

Eventually, Roxanni did venture out into the wider enclosure. She was braver than Rhea had been, trotting right out into the middle of the space and standing there with her tail twitching with excitement. Then she went straight up to the electrified perimeter fence. The electrified fences are designed to discourage cats from climbing, not to actually hurt them, but it was still a surprise for poor Roxanni when she touched it.

By next morning, though, the sisters were more relaxed about their surroundings. They seemed to be getting along well, so Leda was also released that afternoon. To begin with, the old leopardess didn't

budge, but after an hour or so, she sauntered out looking like she owned the place!

Right at the top of their home range, Leda discovered a tree that stood like a parasol to guard against the sun. She eyed the welcoming shade above her head and sniffed the air daintily. Then, with a single powerful leap, she was up in the branches, scattering the surprised birds. It was a clumsy move by leopard standards, but she'd perfect it in time.

Leopards are famously good at climbing trees. They often drag a carcass three times their own weight into a tree and can descend head-first.

FACT FILE

When Leda had enough of the view, she picked her way carefully down to the ground. This was going to be her tree. There was enough of the wild cat left in Leda to bring deep territorial behaviors back to the surface. She walked to the base of the tree and turned around, squirting a few sprays of urine around the trunk. Now what else could she claim? As Leda walked away happily, she curved her tail in the air, higher than ever before.

Leopards are territorial and mark their land with urine, feces, and cheek-rubbing on trees. They also like to scratch to mark their territory. This tells other leopards that might be passing through that the territory is taken.

Gradually, the afternoon gave way to a glorious copper-colored dusk. It was going to be another beautiful Shamwari night.

Chapter Eleven

September 2009
Shamwari Reserve, South Africa

Just a few months after the leopards' arrival,
they were unrecognizable. The Centre and its
surroundings looked different, too. Rain had swept
across the plains and the land was rich and green.
Brightly-colored songbirds called from the scrub and
the air hummed with the drone of insects. The smell
of wet earth and wild flowers filled the air.

In the cats' enclosure, the leopards were awake for
the sunrise. From the edge of the camp, Roxanni and
Rhea were watching warthogs as they dug in the
mud for roots. Leda settled down in a patch of spring
sun as the three of them stared out at their world.

A world of freedom, a long way from the concrete misery they had left behind forever. The Shamwari leopards were home at last.

Afterword

Leda and her daughters settled happily into Shamwari life, but then tragedy struck. In January 2011, Roxanni suddenly went off her food. It was kidney trouble again; a repeat of the problem that she'd developed at Limassol Zoo. At first it seemed she was responding well to the medicine prescribed by Shamwari's veterinary team. Everyone was hopeful that she'd fight her illness, but sadly, it wasn't the case. Roxanni died on February 9th, 2011. Just that morning, one of her caretakers at the Centre had seen her walking along the perimeter fence, enjoying the morning sunshine.

Roxanni had been able to enjoy Shamwari for two years before her illness took her. She had two years to feel grass and dirt under her huge paws instead of bare concrete. Two years of seeing the sun rise and set over her ancestral homeland. Roxanni is sorely missed but, to this day, Leda and Rhea continue to thrive in the comfort and space of Shamwari.

Read all the
rescue stories

BCPL
Baltimore County
Public Library

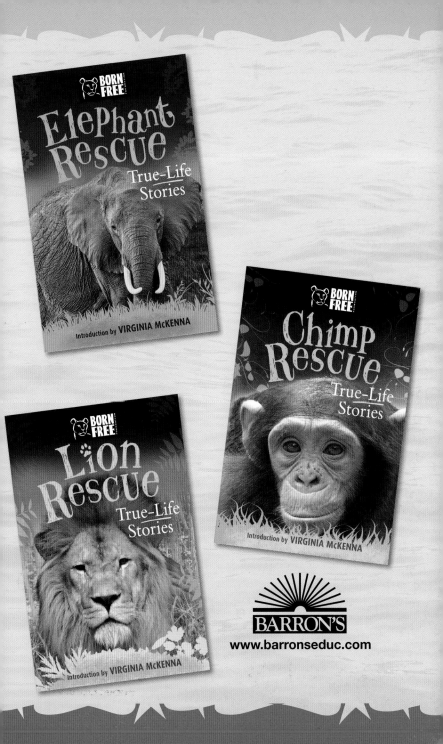

BORN FREE FOUNDATION

Go wild with Born Free

Welcome to the Born Free Foundation, where people get into animals and go wild! Our wildlife charity takes action all around the world to save lions, elephants, gorillas, tigers, chimps, dolphins, bears, wolves, and lots more.

If you're wild about animals, visit
www.bornfreeusa.org
To join our free kids' club, WildcreW, or adopt your own animal, visit **www.bornfree.org.uk**

Keep Wildlife in the Wild